Marriage, Culture, and Scripture

A LOOK AT

GOD'S DESIGN FOR MARRIAGE

Dr. Paul Friesen
Dr. Virginia Friesen

Home Improvement Ministries
Bedford, Massachusetts

MARRIAGE, CULTURE, AND SCRIPTURE: A LOOK AT GOD'S DESIGN FOR MARRIAGE
Copyright © 2012 by Paul and Virginia Friesen

Design and production: Barbara Steele
Copy editing: Guy Steele

ISBN: 978-1-936907-04-5

Published by Home Improvement Ministries.
For information on other H.I.M. resources, please contact:
    Home Improvement Ministries
    213 Burlington Road, Suite 101-B
    Bedford, MA 01730
E-mail inquiries: info@HIMweb.org

Find us on the web at: www.HIMweb.org

All rights reserved. Written permission must be secured from the publisher to use or reproduce any part of this book, except for brief quotations in critical reviews or articles. For information on obtaining permission for reprints and excerpts, contact: permissions@HIMweb.org

Scripture quotations are from The Holy Bible, English Standard Version® (ESV®), copyright © 2001 by Crossway, a publishing ministry of Good News Publishers. Used by permission. All rights reserved.

Printed in the United States of America.   11/12TPS1500

Dedication

To Derek and Julie Johnson and the incredible staff
at the CURE Children's Hospital of Uganda

∽

*Thanks for all you are doing to bring physical
and spiritual healing to so many*

Contents

Foreword 7

Introduction 9

PART ONE / God's Word on Marriage and Relationships

God's Design for Husband and Wife 11

Deceptions from Satan Regarding Marital Intimacy 17

The Discipline Required for Marital Intimacy 21

The Delight in Experiencing Marital Intimacy 25

The Importance of Expressing Love and Respect 27

Honoring God and Each Other in Your Sexual Relationship 37

PART TWO / Practical Questions

Preparing for Marriage 41

Marital Sexuality 45

Parents, In-laws, and Extended Family 49

Finances 51

Divorce 53

Family Planning 55

Marriage and Dowries 59

About the Authors 61

Acknowledgments 63

 Foreword

In *Marriage, Culture, and Scripture*, Paul and Virginia raise universally shared issues that are relevant to every marriage in every nation. They expose the common and subtle distortions of God's word on marriage, and with amazing simplicity, reveal the redemptive truths that will restore the institution of marriage as the most enjoyable gift to man this side of eternity!

Having listened to them present from this material, I highly recommend this fine piece of work for teaching, counseling, and discussions that will lead to Godly marriages and happy families.

Wilberforce Okumu, Senior Pastor
Pearl Haven Christian Center, Mbale, Uganda

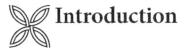 Introduction

It is absolutely critical to believe and be committed to God's word as our guide in how we interact as husband and wife. God's word gives very clear principles for how we are to treat each other.

Most of our marriage issues will become much less problematic when we are each determined to love the Lord and to follow His word fully. What we've written here is what we believe scripture says about the relationship of husband and wife. We encourage you to study God's word to see if this is true. Most importantly, we urge you, whether or not you agree with all we say, to ask God to show you His way and to take care that the decisions you make about how you live as husband and wife are supported by scripture, rather than by emotions, hormones, the advice of friends, or society and culture.

Although we have worked on this booklet as a couple, we will reference Paul as the writer's voice for ease of reading.

PART ONE / God's Word on Marriage and Relationships

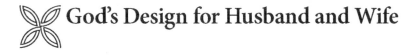 God's Design for Husband and Wife

Then the Lord God said, "It is not good that the man should be alone; I will make him a helper fit for him." Now out of the ground the Lord God had formed every beast of the field and every bird of the heavens and brought them to the man to see what he would call them. And whatever the man called every living creature, that was its name. The man gave names to all livestock and to the birds of the heavens and to every beast of the field. But for Adam there was not found a helper fit for him. So the Lord God caused a deep sleep to fall upon the man, and while he slept took one of his ribs and closed up its place with flesh. And the rib that the Lord God had taken from the man he made into a woman and brought her to the man. Then the man said,

> *"This at last is bone of my bones*
> *and flesh of my flesh;*
> *she shall be called Woman,*
> *because she was taken out of Man."*

Therefore a man shall leave his father and his mother and hold fast to his wife, and they shall become one flesh. And the man and his wife were both naked and were not ashamed. —Genesis 2:18–25

■ It is not good to be alone. We were made for community.

In the perfect setting of Eden, where Adam had a perfect relationship with God and all creation, God says for the first time something is not good. It is not good that Adam is alone, so God creates a partner for him in Eve. Adam named all the animals, and none of them were suited to be his partners because none of them bore the image of God.

It is true that the Apostle Paul says some have the gift of singleness.

> *I wish that all were as I myself am. But each has his own gift from God, one of one kind and one of another.* —1 Corinthians 7:7

It is also true that Jesus speaks of those that have made themselves single for the kingdom's sake:

> *For there are eunuchs who have been so from birth, and there are eunuchs who have been made eunuchs by men, and there are eunuchs who have made themselves eunuchs for the sake of the kingdom of heaven. Let the one who is able to receive this receive it.* —Matthew 19:12

The reality is and the expectation is, however, that most men and women will marry.

> *But if they cannot exercise self-control, they should marry. For it is better to marry than to burn with passion.* —1 Corinthians 7:9

■ A suitable helper was created.

God creates Eve out of Adam. God says He will make a "helper" suitable for him. This in no way implies that Eve was inferior to Adam or below him. We often think of a helper as someone less than or lower than the one they are helping; but here God is saying, "Adam, you need help! You need a partner."

The word "helper" (in Hebrew, *ezer*) is used only 21 times in the Old Testament. Twice it is used to refer to Eve, three times it is used to refer to nations that provided military assistance to Israel, and the other 16 times it is used in reference to God as a helper. All of these verses are talking about a vital, powerful and rescuing kind of help. *Ezer* describes aspects of God's character—He is our strength, our rescuer, our protector, and our help! And *ezer* was the Holy Spirit's choice of word to describe the first woman. Eve was someone who would provide valuable and vital strength and assistance to Adam.

> *Then God said, "Let us make man in our image, after our likeness. And let them have dominion over the fish of the sea and over the birds of the heavens and over the livestock and over all the earth and over every creeping thing that creeps on the earth."*
>
> > *So God created man in his own image,*
> > *in the image of God he created him;*
> > *male and female he created them.*
>
> *And God blessed them. And God said to them, "Be fruitful and multiply and fill the earth and subdue it, and have dominion over the fish of the sea and over the birds of the heavens and over every living thing that moves on the earth."* —Genesis 1:26–28

▨ Being made in the image of God gives *both* man and woman dignity.

We are to treat each other with kindness, dignity, and respect because all humans are created in God's image.

> *There is neither Jew nor Greek, there is neither slave nor free, there is no male and female, for you are all one in Christ Jesus.* —Galatians 3:28

We have value because we are made in the image of God, not because we are better educated, or have the ability to earn more money, or have more prestige in the community, or more physical beauty. Each of us bears the image of God and each of us is "fearfully and wonderfully made":

> *I praise you, for I am fearfully and wonderfully made. Wonderful are your works; my soul knows it very well.* —Psalm 139:14

We are all equal in value before Christ. How we treat each person—husband, wife, children, friends, enemies—is seen as how we treat Christ:

> *"Then they also will answer, saying, 'Lord, when did we see you hungry or thirsty or a stranger or naked or sick or in prison, and did not minister to you?' Then he will answer them, saying, 'Truly, I say to you, as you did not do it to one of the least of these, you did not do it to me'"*
> —Matthew 25:44–45

If we were being unkind to our spouse or children and our pastor walked in, we would cease being unkind. We are able to control our actions depending on how much we value the persons we are interacting with. Well, the pastor may not be in the house, but Jesus is always in the house and He says, the way you treat your spouse and children is the way you are treating me.

▨ Being created in the image of God gives us diversity as well as dignity.

> *So God created man in his own image,*
> *in the image of God he created him;*
> *male and female he created them.*   —Genesis 1:27

The members of the Trinity are all equal to each other, but not the same. The roles of God the Father, God the Son, and God the Holy Spirit are all different, but they are all equally God.

> "Helper fit for him" means "a helper matching his distinctiveness." It certainly points to one who is fit to stand before the man, opposite him, as his counterpart, companion and complement. There is no sense of inferiority, subordination or servitude implied here; rather, it is one who is "like him" but "like opposite him" (to give a literal rendering).
> —Atkinson, *The Message of Genesis 1-11*, p. 69

So it is God who created men and women as equal. This is critical to understand. If we treat men and women differently in the church or give special honor to one over the other we are showing favoritism, which James speaks frankly about:

> *If you really fulfill the royal law according to the Scripture, "You shall love your neighbor as yourself," you are doing well. But if you show partiality, you are committing sin and are convicted by the law as transgressors.*
> —James 2:8-9

It is also God who created us opposite each other: "like" each other in that we are all equal, but "opposite" each other in that we are male or female.

Some of the ways we are different have to do with how we communicate with each other and the ways we view our sexual relationship as husband and wife.

Different in communication

When a husband comes home from work, his wife might ask him to tell her how his day was. "Fine," he says. She may then start asking a series of extremely irritating questions such as, "Well, where did you have lunch?" "Who ate with you?" "What did you have?" "What did you talk about? You must have talked about something!"

No one told the man to say "Fine," or directed the woman to ask a million questions. But God created us this way before the fall (see Genesis 2:18, "helper fit"—literally, "like opposite"). I believe it has to do largely with our wiring as men to be task-oriented and as women to be more relational.

When we understand that it is God who has wired us this way, we can accept and tolerate our differences and the annoyances that often accompany them.

Different in sexual expression

Sex is another area that tends to cause tension in many marriages. It is critical to understand some things about sex. First and foremost: God created sex. He speaks about the sexual relationship between a husband and wife very positively in scripture. Yet He *intentionally* created us very different in this area.

Although it is true that the sexual relationship is to be mutual, we enter this relationship in totally different ways. Men need the physical aspect of sex in order to enter the relational, and women need the relational aspect in order to enter the physical.

Different in personality and temperament

Part of being "fearfully and wonderfully" made, as Psalm 139 tells us, is our different temperaments. The same God who called us into oneness as couples often makes us completely different from one another in our personalities and temperaments.

Some of us enjoy being around a lot of people and actually feel more alive when we are. Others of us enjoy being alone—being around people actually wears us out.

Some of us are more organized and detail-oriented and know where everything is in the home and have a home for everything. Others of us are more visionary; we are not as organized, we think up programs and have lots of ideas—but are not as organized.

We need to be thankful to have a mate who is "fearfully and wonderfully" made in the image of God, rather than attempting to remake him or her in our image. Again, we need to ponder why God made us to be so different when He could have chosen to make us all alike.

These differences were before the fall and God said it was very good.

> *Then God said, "Let us make man in our image, after our likeness. And let them have dominion over the fish of the sea and over the birds of the heavens and over the livestock and over all the earth and over every creeping thing that creeps on the earth." . . . And God saw everything that he had made, and behold, it was very good. And there was evening and there was morning, the sixth day.* —Genesis 1:26, 31

 Deceptions from Satan Regarding Marital Intimacy

Now the serpent was more crafty than any other beast of the field that the Lord God had made.

He said to the woman, "Did God actually say, 'You shall not eat of any tree in the garden'?" And the woman said to the serpent, "We may eat of the fruit of the trees in the garden, but God said, 'You shall not eat of the fruit of the tree that is in the midst of the garden, neither shall you touch it, lest you die.'" But the serpent said to the woman, "You will not surely die. For God knows that when you eat of it your eyes will be opened, and you will be like God, knowing good and evil." So when the woman saw that the tree was good for food, and that it was a delight to the eyes, and that the tree was to be desired to make one wise, she took of its fruit and ate, and she also gave some to her husband who was with her, and he ate. Then the eyes of both were opened, and they knew that they were naked. And they sewed fig leaves together and made themselves loincloths.

—Genesis 3:1–7

Deception #1: "God's word is not authoritative."

"Did God really say, 'You must not eat from any tree in the garden'?"

One of Satan's greatest weapons against us is to get us to doubt God's word as being totally trustworthy.

For the time is coming when people will not endure sound teaching, but having itching ears they will accumulate for themselves teachers to suit their own passions, and will turn away from listening to the truth and wander off into myths. —2 Timothy 4:3–4

Deception #2: "You should follow your cultural traditions over scripture."

> *And he said to them, "You have a fine way of rejecting the commandment of God in order to establish your tradition! . . . thus making void the word of God by your tradition that you have handed down. And many such things you do."* —Mark 7:9, 13

Whenever cultural traditions and scripture collide, scripture should always be followed. This is why it is so important to know God's word.

God is not against cultural expression in applying His word, but is against us ever following cultural traditions that contradict His word.

Deception #3: "You really do not need each other."

> *Then the Lord God said, "It is not good that the man should be alone; I will make him a helper fit for him."* —Genesis 2:18

God desires unity, oneness, harmony, and community. Satan therefore will do all he can to encourage isolation and individualism.

Notice that Satan approached Eve only and didn't ask Adam to join the conversation, even though he was there. Eve's temptation that led to sin was acting independently: "I don't need to check with Adam." Adam's temptation that led to sin was non-involvement, not participating and not protecting.

Deception #4: "Your personal—and immediate—gratification is the most important thing."

> *So when the woman saw that the tree was good for food, and that it was a delight to the eyes, and that the tree was to be desired to make one wise, she took of its fruit and ate, and she also gave some to her husband who was with her, and he ate.* —Genesis 3:6

It is all too easy for us to believe that our immediate happiness is more important than obeying God's word.

Deception #5: "Ignoring God's word will not have lasting negative effects."

But the serpent said to the woman, "You will not surely die. For God knows that when you eat of it your eyes will be opened, and you will be like God, knowing good and evil." —Genesis 3:4–5

Satan wants us to believe that disobeying God's word will not have lasting effects. Even though Adam and Eve did not die physically and may have thought God's word was not true, they did begin to die spiritually and put in motion that which would kill them physically as well. Sometimes when we sin and bad things don't immediately happen, we think that God was not serious and following Him is really not that important.

Deception #6: "Following Satan's lead will lead to a more satisfying life."

With much seductive speech she persuades him;
  with her smooth talk she compels him.
All at once he follows her,
  as an ox goes to the slaughter,
  or as a stag is caught fast
    till an arrow pierces its liver;
  as a bird rushes into a snare;
    he does not know that it will cost him his life.
—Proverbs 7:21–23

Satan is not able to create anything, so he is only able to take what God has given us to enjoy and deceive us into believing that he can give us those joys outside of an obedient relationship to Christ.

Take, for instance, sexuality. God created sex as a gift for married couples to enjoy oneness, unity, intimacy, and pleasure. Satan entices us to believe that we are able to have this pleasure outside of the bounds of a covenant marriage relationship. Our bodies were created in such a way that a sexual relationship also feels pleasurable outside of marriage. The difference is that a sexual relationship outside of marriage always brings grief and destruction to the couple in one way or another.

At the end of Genesis 2, we read that before sin entered the world

  . . . the man and his wife were both naked and were not ashamed.
—Genesis 2:25

At the end of Genesis 3, after Satan has tempted Adam and Eve and they have sinned, we find they are no longer naked, but their bodies are covered with fig leaves. Instead of having a close relationship with God, they are now hiding from God.

Satan said, "I can give you more than God; I can improve on God's design." In the end, after sin, Adam and Eve experienced less pleasure and freedom than before sin. Satan is still using this same temptation. He still tries to get us to believe that we will be better off after listening to his voice. The same result happens when we sin today. We are less close to each other and God, and instead of experiencing more freedom, we are experiencing far less.

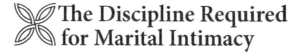The Discipline Required for Marital Intimacy

■ The Discipline of Sacrificial Love

In this is love, not that we have loved God but that he loved us and sent his Son to be the propitiation for our sins. —1 John 4:10

Love is most fully expressed through sacrifice. We know God's love for us most fully though His sacrifice of His Son and His Son's willingness to be obedient to die for our sins.

"For God so loved the world, that he gave his only Son, that whoever believes in him should not perish but have eternal life." —John 3:16

Such sacrificial love is greater than any other expression of love.

In the same way, we most fully feel loved by our spouse when they sacrifice for us.

Love is not first doing what *you* want to do, but knowing your mate's wishes and doing that, especially when that is not what you would naturally choose.

I asked one wife what would make her feel very loved by her husband and she said, "If he would help with the housework."

We need to ask our mate what we could do that would help him or her feel more loved. It is good to listen carefully to things that are their favorites, such as food or drinks, and provide those for them as an act of love.

It takes more than knowing what our mate likes to help them feel loved—it takes doing something with that information. After Jesus washed the disciples' feet, he told them they would be blessed—*if* they did something with that information:

"If you know these things, blessed are you if you do them." —John 13:17

In fact, when we know what our spouse likes and do not do it, it is often more hurtful to them than if we never knew.

Often times our tendency is to do for our spouse what we would like done for us. A wife may make her favorite meal for her husband's birthday because she likes that meal and wants to cook a healthy meal for her husband, instead of thinking what meal he would really like.

> The route to intimacy is a paradox: We must care less about ourselves than we do about our spouse. —Dan Allender, in *Intimate Allies*

▩ The Discipline of Exclusivity

There are two relationships that we are to be exclusive in. One is the relationship with God and the other is the relationship with our spouse.

Exclusivity with God

> "You shall have no other gods before me." —*Exodus 20:3*

> And he said to all, "If anyone would come after me, let him deny himself and take up his cross daily and follow me." —*Luke 9:23*

> "No one can serve two masters, for either he will hate the one and love the other, or he will be devoted to the one and despise the other. You cannot serve God and money." —*Matthew 6:24*

God is very clear that He is not willing to be one of many gods in our life. He is to be *the only god* in our life.

Exclusivity with Spouse

In the same way, our relationship with our spouse is not to be shared with anyone.

> *Then the man said,*
>   *"This at last is bone of my bones*
>   *and flesh of my flesh;*
>   *she shall be called Woman,*
>   *because she was taken out of Man."*
> *Therefore a man shall leave his father and his mother and hold fast to his wife, and they shall become one flesh.* —*Genesis 2:23-24*

The Discipline Required for Marital Intimacy

"But I say to you that everyone who looks at a woman with lustful intent has already committed adultery with her in his heart."
—Matthew 5:28

He answered, "Have you not read that he who created them from the beginning made them male and female, and said, 'Therefore a man shall leave his father and his mother and hold fast to his wife, and the two shall become one flesh'? So they are no longer two but one flesh. What therefore God has joined together, let not man separate."
—Matthew 19:4–6

The *two become one*, not the three or four. God's design is for us to be exclusively committed to our covenant marriage partner for life, and to that person alone.

In order to experience all God has for us in marriage, we must abandon anything that could challenge the exclusivity of the marriage relationship. Nothing should hinder the marriage relationship. It should be our highest priority next to our relationship with the Lord.

Because "they are no longer two but one," all decisions should now be tested by the question, "Is this best for our marriage?" Since the two become one, no major decisions should be made without the husband and wife talking to each other.

The Delight in Experiencing Marital Intimacy

"Whoever seeks to preserve his life will lose it, but whoever loses his life will keep it." —Luke 17:33

But, as it is written,
*   "What no eye has seen, nor ear heard,*
*   nor the heart of man imagined,*
*   what God has prepared for those who love him"—*
*   —1 Corinthians 2:9*

The Irony of Intimacy

The irony of intimacy is that when we put the needs and desires of our spouse ahead of our own, we actually experience more of what we always long for in marriage.

We were designed to put the interests of others before ourselves. And when we live according to God's design, we are more fully who we were created to be and therefore more fulfilled and satisfied.

When we put the desires and needs of our spouse ahead of our own, we will likely find that our spouse responds more warmly to us and to our own desires and needs. We do not do this in a demanding or manipulating way, but as a way of honoring the Lord.

▮ More Than We Ever Could Imagine

God desires to give us more than we ever could imagine, and He is able!

> *Now to him who is able to do far more abundantly than all that we ask or think, according to the power at work within us, to him be glory in the church and in Christ Jesus throughout all generations, forever and ever. Amen.* —*Ephesians 3:20–21*

The problem isn't that we expect too much from God, it is that we don't have any idea how much God wishes to give us when we follow Him.

The Importance of Expressing Love and Respect

Now the serpent was more crafty than any other beast of the field that the LORD God had made.

He said to the woman, "Did God actually say, 'You shall not eat of any tree in the garden'?" And the woman said to the serpent, "We may eat of the fruit of the trees in the garden, but God said, 'You shall not eat of the fruit of the tree that is in the midst of the garden, neither shall you touch it, lest you die.'" But the serpent said to the woman, "You will not surely die. For God knows that when you eat of it your eyes will be opened, and you will be like God, knowing good and evil." So when the woman saw that the tree was good for food, and that it was a delight to the eyes, and that the tree was to be desired to make one wise, she took of its fruit and ate, and she also gave some to her husband who was with her, and he ate. Then the eyes of both were opened, and they knew that they were naked. And they sewed fig leaves together and made themselves loincloths.

—Genesis 3:1–7

God said it was not good for man to be alone—so Satan immediately tempted Eve to act alone. Instead of Eve asking Adam "who was with her" to remind her of what God had said, she acted independently and did not ask her husband to help her, even though it was to her husband that God had given the instructions. She even misspoke about God's direction when she told the serpent God said she was not to even touch the tree. God said not to eat of the tree; He said nothing about touching it.

Adam, instead of providing correct information and protecting Eve from the serpent, was disengaged, not paying attention to his wife, even though she was right beside him.

Eve's sin was acting independently of Adam and not engaging him. Women often do this today, feeling they are right and don't need the perspective of their husbands. Men tend to not engage with their wives and often are not there to partner with them and to protect them.

The effects of sin on all husbands and wives

Before sin entered the world, Adam and Eve lived in perfect harmony in the Garden. They were "like but opposite" each other and used their differences to "rule over all the earth" as a couple with unity.

When sin entered the world though the disobedience of Adam and Eve, the differences between them that were meant to bring delight instead brought disharmony and conflict.

Part of the way sin has affected men and women is that they tend to resist taking responsibility for their own actions; instead they try to blame others for their own actions.

> *And they heard the sound of the LORD God walking in the garden in the cool of the day, and the man and his wife hid themselves from the presence of the LORD God among the trees of the garden. But the LORD God called to the man and said to him, "Where are you?" And he said, "I heard the sound of you in the garden, and I was afraid, because I was naked, and I hid myself." He said, "Who told you that you were naked? Have you eaten of the tree of which I commanded you not to eat?" The man said, "The woman whom you gave to be with me, she gave me fruit of the tree, and I ate." Then the LORD God said to the woman, "What is this that you have done?" The woman said, "The serpent deceived me, and I ate."* —Genesis 3:8–13

The role of submission, respect, and love in the marriage relationship

Most of scripture is not directed specifically to men and women, but here God speaks directly to men and women as to the result of their sin.

And to Adam he said,
> "Because you have listened to the voice of your wife
> and have eaten of the tree
> of which I commanded you,
> 'You shall not eat of it,'
> cursed is the ground because of you;
> in pain you shall eat of it all the days of your life;
> thorns and thistles it shall bring forth for you;
> and you shall eat the plants of the field.
> By the sweat of your face
> you shall eat bread,
> till you return to the ground,
> for out of it you were taken;
> for you are dust,
> and to dust you shall return."   —Genesis 3:17–19

The failure of Adam is that he knew what was best for his wife, but he listened to her and followed her in disobeying God's commands instead of leading her in God's way.

As a result of his sin, his work, which had been a joy, has now become a toil. The land, which before produced only good plants, now produces weeds.

God also spoke to Eve:

> To the woman he said,
> "I will surely multiply your pain in childbearing;
> in pain you shall bring forth children.
> Your desire shall be for your husband,
> and he shall rule over you."   —Genesis 3:16

Before sin, a woman could give birth to children without pain. Now childbirth is painful. The verse also says women will have a desire for their husbands, but their husbands will rule over them.

It is important to understand the word "desire" here. There are at least three interpretations that I know of:

1. Some people believe it means that, as a result of the fall, women will want a sexual relationship with their husbands, but their husbands will rule over them. However, I seldom find men complaining that their wives want sex all the time, so this must not be what it means.

2. Many people believe it means that, as a result of the fall, women will have a desire for an intimate relationship with their husbands, but their husbands will rule over them. It is true that God wants us to have a close relationship with our spouse, but that is not what is being talked about here. In the next chapter of Genesis this same phrase is used:

> *"If you do well, will you not be accepted? And if you do not do well, sin is crouching at the door. Its desire is for you, but you must rule over it."* —Genesis 4:7

Sin and Satan have no desire for a close relationship with you. All they want to do is to control you. Therefore, if you take this back to Genesis 3:16, you come to the third interpretation:

3. Because of the fall, women's tendency will be to attempt to control their husbands, and their husbands will attempt to rule over them. This interpretation makes sense. I have heard many husbands complain that their wives are always correcting them, telling them how they should or could have done better. They try to control their husbands, not physically, but verbally, nagging and complaining and trying to change their husbands.

Husbands, on the other hand, instead of protecting and caring for their wives, have ruled over them and neglected their role as protectors and caretakers. Many have even withdrawn or abandoned their wives, then come back and tried to force them to do what they want through rage, anger, or intimidation.

It is critical to understand that what God is talking about in these verses, addressed to both husband and wife, is associated with the curse that resulted from sin. In no way is any of this a blessing. "He will rule over you" is neither a blessing to the woman nor to the man. It is not how God desires it to be.

We know this to be true because the other major portion of scripture directed specifically to men and women is found in the Apostle Paul's letter to the Ephesians:

> *Wives, submit to your own husbands, as to the Lord. For the husband is the head of the wife even as Christ is the head of the church, his body, and is himself its Savior. Now as the church submits to Christ, so also wives should submit in everything to their husbands.*

> *Husbands, love your wives, as Christ loved the church and gave himself up for her, that he might sanctify her, having cleansed her by the washing of water with the word, so that he might present the church to himself in splendor, without spot or wrinkle or any such thing, that she might be holy and without blemish. In the same way husbands should love their wives as their own bodies. He who loves his wife loves himself. For no one ever hated his own flesh, but nourishes and cherishes it, just as Christ does the church, because we are members of his body. "Therefore a man shall leave his father and mother and hold fast to his wife, and the two shall become one flesh." This mystery is profound, and I am saying that it refers to Christ and the church. However, let each one of you love his wife as himself, and let the wife see that she respects her husband.*
> —Ephesians 5:22–33

Remarkably, here we see that the Apostle Paul, under the guidance of the Holy Spirit, is describing the antidote to the fall:

Husbands, because of the fall your tendency is to rule over your wives; love them by serving them.

Wives, because of the fall your tendency is to control your husbands; love them by respecting and submitting to them.

Paul does *not* say, "Now, you all love and respect each other." He specifically tells husbands to love and wives to submit and respect.

These commands are independent and unconditional. It does not say, "Husbands, love your wife *if* your wife is nice" or "*unless* your wife is mean to you."

It does not say, "Wives, submit to and respect your husbands *if* he treats you the way you think he should" or "*unless* he does not treat you the way you imagined he would."

When husbands love their wives and wives respect and submit to their husbands, they have the greatest possibility of getting back to what God designed marriage to be in Eden.

Let's consider the specific roles and responsibilities of husbands and wives in carrying out these commands.

The passage starts by saying that the husband is the authority in the home:

> *For the husband is the head of the wife even as Christ is the head of the church . . .* —Ephesians 5:23a

This means that the husband has been given authority over the wife. Many a man simply hears, "For the husband is the head of the wife" and then closes the Bible and says, "That's enough Bible for today." He then goes on to think that if he is the head of the wife, that is like the boss, and everyone should be there to serve him. Not quite! Read the next sentence: "For the husband is the head of the wife even as Christ is the head of the church." Christ does have authority over the church. No one ever is confused thinking the Church has authority over Christ; nor should one think the wife has authority over her husband. *But,* before you take a breath, remember that Christ *never used his authority for his selfish ends.* Christ always used his authority to do whatever was best for his bride, the Church.

It is critical here to acknowledge that the position of authority and primary responsibility in the home is positional. That means it is assigned by God, not "earned" because one is smarter, earns more money, etc.

▓ Husbands are called to do four things:

1. Be the chief servant.

> *Husbands, love your wives, as Christ loved the church and gave himself up for her . . .*   —Ephesians 5:25

Christ was the Chief servant. He only uses His authority to serve.

> *"For even the Son of Man came not to be served but to serve, and to give his life as a ransom for many."*   —Mark 10:45

Both husbands and wives are to serve each other, but the husband is to use his authority to serve his wife and family. For too long, men have seen their wives as the ones to serve them rather than the husband as the chief servant.

Very practically, let's say the family is eating a meal and having a chicken. In the typical family, the food is put in front of the husband as the head of the family, and he takes the best piece of meat and passes on to the other members of the family. In the Christian family, I would suggest that the father, because he is the head of the family and has authority, takes the platter and passes it to his wife, she takes some and passes it to their children, and he gets what is left, because he has authority to serve his family first.

2. Lead your family.

Christ took initiative with the church and led the church. Too many men become "Whatever you wish, dear" men and never lead or are missing altogether from the home.

> And Jesus called them to him and said to them, "You know that those who are considered rulers of the Gentiles lord it over them, and their great ones exercise authority over them. But it shall not be so among you. But whoever would be great among you must be your servant..."
> —Mark 10:42-43

3. Take spiritual initiative.

Jesus cleansed the Church by the washing with water through the word. We as husbands are called to be spiritual leaders in our home. That certainly does not mean we need to know more or be more educated, but what it does mean is that we take the initiative in our home to lead our family spiritually. It could start with making sure we give thanks before each meal, making sure we are all in church on Sunday, and reading the Bible in our homes. Our wives should not be pulling the family along spiritually.

4. Help her become more radiant.

Jesus interacted with the church, to present her to himself as a radiant church, without stain or wrinkle or any other blemish, but holy and blameless. I am not sure about all that this means, but I know that part of my role as a husband is to help my wife become more and more radiant. One of the ways I do this is by knowing her dreams and desires, her gifts and abilities, so that I can help her become all she can be. It may mean staying home with the children so she can take a class or go to a study or just relax. Too often, our wives are worn out because they have taken care of us instead of us taking care of them.

▓ Wives are called to do two things:

1. Submit to your husbands.

It is very important that we understand submission does not mean lack of equality. Remember, our example is the relationship of the Trinity. In Jesus we find the model for both the husband and the wife. The husband is to love his wife as Christ loved the Church, and the wife is to submit to her husband as Christ submitted to God the Father. The most vivid account is of that moment in the Garden of Gethsemane when Jesus reasons with the Father and asks if there might be another way to accomplish the salvation of the world; yet He submits to the Father's plan.

> *And he withdrew from them about a stone's throw, and knelt down and prayed, saying, "Father, if you are willing, remove this cup from me. Nevertheless, not my will, but yours, be done."* —Luke 22:41–42

Jesus' submission to the Father in no way made Him less than the Father.

Jesus' obedience to the will of the Father also did not make Him less than the Father.

> *"I glorified you on earth, having accomplished the work that you gave me to do."* —John 17:4

So in the marriage relationship, submission does not mean a lack of full interaction and contribution from the wife. It does mean that after full interaction is given, unless the husband is asking the wife to do something specifically forbidden in scripture, she is to submit to the husband's decision.

Given the tendency for wives to try to control their husbands as a result of the fall, we like the definition of submission that Larry Crabb gives.

"Submission is resisting the urge to control." —Larry Crabb

> I cannot give logical arguments for submission. It defies logic that Jesus would release all the glories of heaven so He could give us the glory of heaven. Submission is not about logic; it is about love.
>
> Jesus loved us so much that He voluntarily submitted to death on a cross. His command is that wives are to submit to their husbands. It is a gift that we voluntarily give to the man we have vowed to love in obedience to the Savior we love. . . .
>
> God said that man needs a helper. The true woman celebrates this calling and becomes affirming rather than adversarial, compassionate rather than controlling, a partner rather than a protagonist. She becomes substantively rather than superficially submissive.
>
> The true woman is not afraid to place herself in a position of submission. She does not have to grasp; she does not have to control. Her fear dissolves in the light of God's covenant promise to be her God and to live within her. Submission is simply a demonstration of her confidence in the sovereign power of the Lord God. Submission is a reflection of her redemption. —*The True Woman*, Hunt, pp. 218, 223

2. Respect your husband.

Even though we often talk more about submission, perhaps respect is the more difficult one to fully understand. When a woman tries to control her husband or overrule his decisions, he tends to feel disrespected. Often a woman feels she is trying to "improve" her husband, but he is feeling disrespected.

When Virginia and I are driving together, sometimes she will take it upon herself to "help me drive better." A wife might say things like "Watch out for that pothole! Don't you think you should slow down?" or "Be careful! You almost hit that boda boda!" Instead of feeling helped, the man "hears" in her questions the implication, "You don't know what you are doing."

Cynthia Heald puts it well:

> Some ways I tended to show disrespect for him were to challenge his decisions and, more often than not, to offer my alternatives to those decisions. I would interrupt and correct him in front of others, especially in front of the children. In my effort to inspire him to be his very best, I would give him my lecture entitled, "Whatever you do, it's just not good enough." He could be home more, he could spend more time with the children, he could read more, he could be more sensitive, he could be more spiritual.
>
> One day it dawned on me that I was not Jack's personal Holy Spirit. My job was to respect him and to fulfill my God-given role in our marriage. I was not given to Jack to redo him, but to complement him. When I finally became aware of the log in my eye, I was able to back off and begin to give him time and encouragement to lead. He, then, slowly but confidently became the head of our home.
>
> I have learned that as I respect Jack, I am not so inclined to manipulate him. My respect for Jack was necessary to free him to be the husband and father he was meant to be.   —*Loving Your Husband*, Heald, pp. 50–51

It is important to note that loving your wife and respecting and submitting to your husband are both commands. Therefore, they cannot be simply responses to emotions, but are decisions of the will.

◈ The benefit of responding to God's directions

- Husbands who are respected are more likely to become all God designed them to be.
- Husbands who are respected tend to cherish their wives more fully.
- Wives who are cherished by their husbands are more likely to become all God designed them to be.
- Wives who are cherished tend to show respect to their husbands more fully.
- When husbands and wives do what God has designed them to do, both will find more of the joy and intimacy they have longed for.

Honoring God and Each Other in Your Sexual Relationship

> *So God created man in his own image,*
> *in the image of God he created him;*
> *male and female he created them.*
>
> *And God blessed them. And God said to them, "Be fruitful and multiply and fill the earth and subdue it, and have dominion over the fish of the sea and over the birds of the heavens and over every living thing that moves on the earth."* —Genesis 1:27–28
>
> *And the man and his wife were both naked and were not ashamed.*
> —Genesis 2:25

God has designed us as sexual beings.

It was God who created us as sexual beings. As God, He could have accomplished procreation any way He wished, yet He chose to do it through the sexual union of a husband and wife.

God was the one that chose to create us as male and female rather than male and male or female and female. When God rested on the seventh day and said it was very good, it included our sexuality.

Marriage, Culture, and Scripture

▨ God's word speaks openly and positively about sexual expression in marriage.

> *I came to my garden, my sister, my bride,*
> *I gathered my myrrh with my spice,*
> *I ate my honeycomb with my honey,*
> *I drank my wine with my milk.*
> *Eat, friends, drink,*
> *and be drunk with love!* —Song of Solomon 5:1

This passage is speaking of God looking down on a husband and wife making love and encouraging them to enjoy His gift.

▨ God has designed us physiologically to receive physical pleasure in the act of making love.

Both men and women have sexual organs that have been designed exclusively for sexual arousal and pleasure. God, as Creator, would not create anything that could not be used to glorify Him. Every part of us can be used to honor or dishonor God, but it would not make sense for Him to create any part of us that could only be used to dishonor Him.

> *Let your fountain be blessed,*
> *and rejoice in the wife of your youth,*
> *a lovely deer, a graceful doe.*
> *Let her breasts fill you at all times with delight;*
> *be intoxicated always in her love.* —Proverbs 5:18–19

▨ Regular sexual involvement between husband and wife is the Biblical expectation with mutual benefit.

> *The husband should give to his wife her conjugal rights, and likewise the wife to her husband. For the wife does not have authority over her own body, but the husband does. Likewise the husband does not have authority over his own body, but the wife does. Do not deprive one another, except perhaps by agreement for a limited time, that you may devote yourselves to prayer; but then come together again, so that Satan may not tempt you because of your lack of self-control.*
> —1 Corinthians 7:3–5

Husbands and wives will need to decide together what "regular" means to them, but God's clear direction to husbands and wives is to come together regularly in sexual union.

▨ There is great freedom for erotic expression.

> *Come, my beloved,*
>   *let us go out into the fields*
>   *and lodge in the villages;*
> *let us go out early to the vineyards*
>   *and see whether the vines have budded,*
> *whether the grape blossoms have opened*
>   *and the pomegranates are in bloom.*
> *There I will give you my love.*
> *The mandrakes give forth fragrance,*
>   *and beside our doors are all choice fruits,*
> *new as well as old,*
>   *which I have laid up for you, O my beloved.*
>
> —*Song of Solomon 7:11–13*

Here the wife is taking initiative in inviting the husband out for a trip that will involve "new and old" forms of lovemaking. The passage demonstrates the freedom in location and expression in lovemaking for the married couple. The questions a couple needs to ponder have to do with:

1. Is it prohibited in scripture? If scripture forbids it, a couple should not participate in it. For instance, you would never have anyone else involved other than your spouse. You would not involve blue movies or pornography in your lovemaking.

2. Is it beneficial to the relationship? Making love is meant to bring us together, not push us apart. Does the activity enhance your relationship?

3. Is it harmful physically? Eliminate and avoid anything that would be hurtful or harmful to either of you.

4. Is it mutually agreed upon? This is so important. Making love is to be loving, which means not forced in any way. If one party is not comfortable with a form of sexual expression, then the other should not force it on his or her spouse.

▣ The sexual relationship is to be a lifelong adventure.

> *Let your fountain be blessed,*
>   *and rejoice in the wife of your youth,*
>   *a lovely deer, a graceful doe.*
> *Let her breasts fill you at all times with delight;*
>   *be intoxicated always in her love.*   —*Proverbs 5:18–19*

The sexual relationship, connecting physically, should be something the married couple enjoy for their whole relationship. The physical expression may change with age, but the emotional and physical connection should continue to grow.

PART TWO / Practical Questions

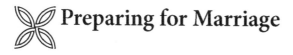 Preparing for Marriage

■ How do I know whom to marry?

The Bible is clear that if one is a Christian, he or she should only marry another Christian:

> Do not be unequally yoked with unbelievers. For what partnership has righteousness with lawlessness? Or what fellowship has light with darkness? —2 Corinthians 6:14

It does not matter how wealthy he is or how beautiful she is, or how intelligent a prospective spouse may be. The most important ingredient in a good marriage is for both of you to be followers of Jesus.

Secondly, only marry someone who believes God's word and is committed to following it.

Thirdly, marry someone who lives a Godly life. He or she should follow God's word and be truthful, kind, loving, etc.

Fourthly, marry someone who has goals and interests similar to your own in life. Say, for instance, you want to go to university and become a nurse, and your prospective husband has no interest in school and has never had a good job. Is this the man you want to be the example to your children? Do you really have that much in common?

Lastly, do you have a romantic attraction to each other, and have you honored God with it in your relationship? This goes back to our previous points about believing God's word and living a Godly life. If he says he loves God and His word but wants you to sleep with him before you are married, I would have serious doubts. If his hormones overrule scripture before marriage, they likely will after marriage as well, and you will have an unfaithful spouse on your hands.

❋ I have heard you are not supposed to have sex before marriage, but what about everything else? Isn't it good to experiment to see if you are sexually compatible?

We often think of sexual compatibility having to do with body parts. Pretty much all the body parts fit. What is much more important is how the relationship fits. Couples that truly love each other will work out any initial awkwardness in their sexual relationship over time. Couples that might have "great sex" before marriage but do not connect relationally will have many more challenges.

Regarding physical involvement, three times in the Song of Solomon, the exact same directions are given by Solomon's wife to her single friends:

> "I adjure you, O daughters of Jerusalem,
> by the gazelles or the does of the field,
> that you not stir up or awaken love
> until it pleases." —Song of Solomon 2:7, 3:5, and 8:4

What this passage is saying is that those who are single are not to arouse each other sexually. God has so designed the body that sexual arousal is used to prepare the body for sexual intercourse, which is reserved for marriage. Anything stopping before completion of the sexual act will be somewhat frustrating because our bodies were not designed to stop after arousal starts. God's design is that they are not to culminate in sexual intercourse until they are married, thus they are not to engage in any form of arousal unless they are married. Another very practical aspect of this is that our bodies are not satisfied to stop short of intercourse, so each time we are together we tend to inch closer to sexual union.

❋ I have heard from many of my married friends that their expectations for marriage were much higher than what they experienced in marriage. How can you help me from being disappointed in marriage?

The first question is: Who or what is shaping your expectations for marriage? A man came home from his honeymoon disappointed in the sexual aspect of the honeymoon. It was discovered that his expectations for how his wife would respond to him were based on movies he had watched that were pornographic in nature.

Others go into marriage thinking marriage is all about making them happy, and they are disappointed when they realize that if two selfish people marry, each expecting the other one to meet all their needs and desires, someone will be disappointed—likely, both.

It is important to go to scripture and see what marriage is designed to be. It is a wonderful relationship, but Jesus makes it clear that marriage is hard and is not for everyone:

> He answered, "Have you not read that he who created them from the beginning made them male and female, and said, 'Therefore a man shall leave his father and his mother and hold fast to his wife, and the two shall become one flesh'? So they are no longer two but one flesh. What therefore God has joined together, let not man separate." They said to him, "Why then did Moses command one to give a certificate of divorce and to send her away?" He said to them, "Because of your hardness of heart Moses allowed you to divorce your wives, but from the beginning it was not so. And I say to you: whoever divorces his wife, except for sexual immorality, and marries another, commits adultery."
>
> The disciples said to him, "If such is the case of a man with his wife, it is better not to marry." But he said to them, "Not everyone can receive this saying, but only those to whom it is given. For there are eunuchs who have been so from birth, and there are eunuchs who have been made eunuchs by men, and there are eunuchs who have made themselves eunuchs for the sake of the kingdom of heaven. Let the one who is able to receive this receive it." 　　—Matthew 19:4–12

Talk to some married folks and see what marriage is really like. Make sure you carefully observe your future mate in all situations so you have a clear picture of the real person you are marrying, and not just the picture he or she wants you to see.

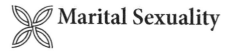
Marital Sexuality

▪ My husband calls himself a Christian, but he beats me and the children when he is angry with us. What do I do?

The first thing to say is that God has created every man, woman, and child in His image, and therefore we must treat each person with dignity. The Bible says, "as we have done to the least of these, so we have done to Christ."

We understand that some are actually advised by their matrons and best-men that beating your wife soon after marriage is an indication of your love for her. But love is always doing what is best for your spouse and that which is loving and sacrificial. Love is always shown voluntarily, not as a response of fear.

If you and your husband attend a healthy church, you should go to the pastor or leaders and ask them to speak to your husband. If they will not, or if he will not stop beating you and/or your children, you should separate and find a safe place to live until your husband is willing to change his sinful behavior. If he refuses to stop this behavior, you are free to divorce him because of his hardness of heart and the damage he is inflicting on you.

It is very important, however, to make sure you are not acting in a way that makes it hard for him to love you. You are still called to treat him in a respectful manner and to submit to his leadership unless it goes against God's word.

▪ My husband tells me that he needs to have sex every day—sometimes many times a day. When I tell him I am not in the mood, he forces me to have sex with him. What should I do?

First, it is important to remember that the sexual relationship between husband and wife was a gift to couples from God to help them experience pleasure, closeness, unity, and joy. Satan is the one that attempts to make our sexual relationship a source of tension. So first, sex is a gift from God to couples—God thought of it. Second, it is true that God has created men to be visually stimulated sexually, to be aroused quickly, and in general, to desire sex more frequently. However, this is never an excuse for the husband to sin in this area. A man will not die if he goes without sex for a week, or a month, or even a year. Remember that the sexual relationship should never be forced. Forced sex is rape, even in the marriage relationship. There is no set amount of sex that a married couple should have, but it should be agreed upon and not forced.

If he continues to force you against your will, you should talk to a trusted counselor or pastor with your husband to help you work this out.

▧ What should a man do if his wife is never in the mood for sex and says she doesn't like it, and he knows he is not to force her to have sex with him?

The husband first needs to ask why the wife is never in the mood. Perhaps he is rough with her and sex hurts her, or she works so hard that she is exhausted at the end of the day. The husband needs to make sure he is helping his wife around the house so she is not so tired. He also needs to realize that for a woman, the desire for sex comes through an emotional connection, while a man is aroused more by visual stimulation. A husband is to serve his wife, and not just so she will be sexually involved with him; but it is also true that a wife who is cared for is often more sexually interested in her husband.

The wife needs to remember that love is often sacrificial, doing that which you mate desires even when you do not. Wives need to ask God to help them be willing to serve their husband's sexual desires even when it is not first theirs. Most men would love it if their wives would take some initiative sexually.

▧ When I was in the late stage of my pregnancy and also very soon after giving birth, I wanted to please my husband sexually, but he demanded sexual intercourse. What do I do?

Again, sexual intercourse is never to be forced. A loving husband would want to be sensitive to his wife's desires and needs.

You should consult a medical expert to see when it is safe to be sexually intimate during and after a pregnancy.

I appreciate that you want to please your husband. There are various ways that you may bring sexual pleasure to him without penetration. One would be to simply experience the pleasure of being naked together and enjoying each other's bodies in this way. Scripture says,

> *Let your fountain be blessed,*
> *and rejoice in the wife of your youth,*
> *a lovely deer, a graceful doe.*
> *Let her breasts fill you at all times with delight;*
> *be intoxicated always in her love.* —Proverbs 5:18-19

We believe this delight in each other's bodies does not always need to be expressed in sexual intercourse.

▪ My husband is sleeping with other women and yet insists on having sexual intercourse with me. I fear he is HIV+. What should I do?

If your husband is sleeping with other women, you must not have sex with him. If he says he will beat you or harm you, you must separate from him until he is he has been tested for sexual diseases, stops sleeping with other women, and lives faithfully with you.

If you as a wife have contributed to his "frustration" by not being intimate, you need to ask God to help you love your husband in this way if he returns to you in fidelity. This is never an excuse for his actions, but regular sexual involvement for married couples is a scriptural expectation:

> *Do not deprive one another, except perhaps by agreement for a limited time, that you may devote yourselves to prayer; but then come together again, so that Satan may not tempt you because of your lack of self-control.* —1 Corinthians 7:5

▪ I am a Christian single person. I slept with a woman who is not a Christian, and now she is pregnant. Her parents tell me I must marry her. What should I do?

First, you should confess your sin to God and to this woman and her family, explaining that what you did was sinful and against everything that God's word says as to how a Christian should live.

Secondly, you should take financial responsibility for this child since you are the father. I realize you may be asked to compensate the family for their time and expense, since the woman is their daughter.

Thirdly, I do not believe you should marry her, as she is not a Christian and scripture is clear on a believer not marrying a non-believer:

> *Do not be unequally yoked with unbelievers. For what partnership has righteousness with lawlessness? Or what fellowship has light with darkness?* —2 Corinthians 6:14

If she refuses to raise the child, you should raise the child yourself or find a loving home for the child. The child should not suffer anymore because of your sinful actions.

If you repent, however, God will forgive you and bless your life as you live in obedience to Him.

How do I know if someone is impotent or not unless I sleep with him?

Scripture gives the sequence for sexual oneness in marriage:

> *Therefore a man shall leave his father and his mother and hold fast to his wife, and they shall become one flesh.* —Genesis 2:24

First, you are to leave mother and father, meaning to become independent from them. Second, you are to be united in marriage. Thirdly, you are to become one. So God clearly says you are to marry before experimenting sexually.

Now, you certainly can tell if a man is able to have sex before marriage by whether he can be aroused sexually. Does the girl have any sexual desire for her boyfriend? She can know this as well. If the real concern is whether he is able to father a child or she is able to become pregnant, and that is critical to the marriage decision, you can seek medical tests to help you understand this, but even then there are no guarantees. You must make sure you are marrying this person because you love him or her, regardless of whether or not they are able to produce children with you.

It is absolutely critical that you share with your future spouse if you know you are not able to have children. You should never hide such information.

Parents, In-laws, and Extended Family

■ **My parents-in-law are ruining our family. They tell my husband what to do and he does it. They demand the money I make, and my husband listens to them. They all treat me like property instead of family. What do I do?**

Ask God to fill you with His Spirit and His love for the family. God desires to show His power to bring healing in all relationships.

Scripture is clear, however, that a man is to leave his mother and father:

> *Therefore a man shall leave his father and his mother and hold fast to his wife, and they shall become one flesh.* —Genesis 2:24

The word leave means to cut, sever, abandon. It does not mean to abandon relationship, but primary allegiance. Children are called to obey their parents, but adults are called to honor them. So you should talk to your husband about God's design. If he and his parents do not agree, you must ask God to help you be the wife he has called you to be. If your husband refuses to put you ahead of his parents and treats you in a harmful way, you should ask your church leaders for advice. Seek God for peace about separating, but only if harm is being done to you.

■ **What is the proper relationship between children and their parents after the children marry?**

Scripture is clear that a man is to leave his mother and father:

> *Therefore a man shall leave his father and his mother and hold fast to his wife, and they shall become one flesh.* —Genesis 2:24

The word leave means to cut, sever, abandon. It does not mean to abandon relationship, but primary allegiance. Children are called to obey their parents, but adults are called to honor them. So after marriage the husband and wife are the unit that should make all decisions that affect their new family. They often are wise to seek counsel from their parents, but they are not required to obey their parents. Adult children are to care for their parents out of love, but not out of requirement from the parents. Again, the first responsibility of the husband is to his wife and children, and the first responsibility of the wife is to her husband and children over his or her parents.

My boyfriend and I are both Christians and want to marry. My parents do not like the man and say I cannot marry. What do we do? I want their blessing.

It is important to have the blessing of your families before you marry. The first thing is to ask your parents why they are opposed to the marriage. Listen carefully to hear truth in what they say. Perhaps you need to wait a bit so they are able to see how responsible your boyfriend is. If your parents are not believers and don't want you to marry a Christian, you need to consider what it means to leave mother and father before marriage. If your parents do not want you to marry a Christian, in essence they are saying they will never allow you to marry unless you marry a non-believer, which you cannot do. In this case you need to decide if you are willing to marry, knowing it may cost you your relationship with your parents. Again, if you decide to marry, you are still called to be respectful of your parents, even when you go against their wishes.

 # Finances

▧ My husband does not work, but expects me to provide for the family while he does nothing. What should I do?

Ask God to help you have a humble spirit as you relate to your husband. It is easy for a woman to become arrogant when she is the "earner." You are still called to submit to and respect your husband in all areas you are able. However, scripture says that if a man does not work, he should not eat:

> For even when we were with you, we would give you this command: If anyone is not willing to work, let him not eat.   —2 Thessalonians 3:10

This passage certainly does not apply when the man is not able to work, but it does apply when the man refuses to work. The leaders in your church should be able to help you understand both why your husband isn't working and how you can encourage him to work. This does not mean nagging your husband, but rather trying to help him in any way you are able.

If your husband refuses to work, you may ultimately need to tell him that if he refuses to work you will separate and take the money you make with you—and he will have to live on his own until he is willing to participate in providing for the family.

Be sure to surround yourself with Godly mentors who are able to encourage you both in God's ways.

▧ Since I make more money than my husband, shouldn't I be able to make the decisions regarding how our money is spent?

When two individuals marry, the two become *one*:

> ". . . So they are no longer two but one flesh. What therefore God has joined together, let not man separate."   —Matthew 19:6

All that the couple earns and owns should now be in one place, and the couple should make the decisions together on how the money is spent, regardless of who makes more.

◾ My husband spends our money on himself and does not talk to me about it. Our children are going hungry and have many needs. What should I do?

The Bible says that if a man does not provide for his family, he is worse than an unbeliever:

> But if anyone does not provide for his relatives, and especially for members of his household, he has denied the faith and is worse than an unbeliever. —1 Timothy 5:8

If your husband is a believer, other men in the church should talk to him. But first consider carefully whether he is indeed spending the money selfishly, and not just differently than you would. Again, you should be talking together about all your money issues.

If your children continue to be in need because they are neglected by their father, you may need to separate yourself so you are able to provide for them without your husband spending the family money on himself.

Again, seek counsel from wise men and women in the church, and be willing to forgive your husband if he responds to counsel.

◾ Since the man is the "head of the home," shouldn't he be the one to handle all the finances?

Since the husband is responsible for the family, he should make the final decisions regarding finances. However, as in all matters of family life, he should not make decisions without input from his wife. There are many cases where the wife has more financial expertise or is more detail-oriented and should be the one listened to or the one balancing the books. Regardless of who is better at finances, since they are one, they make these decisions together. Many couples have set an amount above which they will not spend without each other's knowledge.

 # Divorce

▨ What does the Bible say about divorce in a culture where so much evil is present?

The Bible speaks to every culture in every time period the same about divorce. Some cultures have viewed it differently, but God's word is the same.

Again, it is critical that you look to scripture's view on divorce, not simply to your culture's view.

> "For the man who does not love his wife but divorces her, says the Lord, the God of Israel, covers his garment with violence, says the Lord of hosts. So guard yourselves in your spirit, and do not be faithless."
> —Malachi 2:16

First of all, God hates divorce—for many reasons. It damages God's design for the family and for imparting His word and values to the next generation, not to mention the questions it raises about God's power at work in His children if they can't get along. So God is always for marriage, but does make provision to protect His children from evil.

Scripture gives two specific reasons that divorce is allowed, and in addition makes one more general statement. Jesus states that divorce is permitted for "sexual immorality."

> "And I say to you: whoever divorces his wife, except for sexual immorality, and marries another, commits adultery." —Matthew 19:9

This is to mean divorce is permitted—not required, but permitted—especially if the immorality is repeated or not repented of. The second specific reason divorce is allowed is for desertion of the marriage:

> But if the unbelieving partner separates, let it be so. In such cases the brother or sister is not enslaved. God has called you to peace.
> —1 Corinthians 7:15

The general observation is made by Jesus when he states that Moses allowed divorce because of hardness of hearts:

> *He said to them, "Because of your hardness of heart Moses allowed you to divorce your wives, but from the beginning it was not so."*
> —Matthew 19:8

What was happening in Moses' time was that men were casting off their wives, deserting them, but not giving them a certificate of divorce, without which they could not remarry, thus depriving them of a main source of provision.

Again, God's best is never to divorce. Divorce should never be entered into hastily or without counsel from Godly people, but it is allowed when that which is being done or not done in the marriage is destructive to the members of the family.

These scripture passages do not justify divorce on the basis of hurt feelings, or a man not making as much money as the wife thought he would, or the woman not being as sexually interested as the husband would like.

It is talking about cases where the husband has run out on the family, or where there is beating of the spouse or children, or where there is unrepentant sexual involvement with another man or woman.

Family Planning

Since the Bible says that God opens the womb and closes the womb, is it acceptable for Christians to do any form of family planning?

First of all, there is no place in scripture where we are told how many children to have. But scripture does make mention of the great gift of children. The Psalmist speaks of the heritage of children:

> *Behold, children are a heritage from the Lord,*
>   *the fruit of the womb a reward.*
> *Like arrows in the hand of a warrior*
>   *are the children of one's youth.*
> *Blessed is the man*
>   *who fills his quiver with them!*
> *He shall not be put to shame*
>   *when he speaks with his enemies in the gate.* —Psalm 127:3–5

God spoke to Adam and Eve concerning children:

> *And God blessed them. And God said to them, "Be fruitful and multiply and fill the earth and subdue it, and have dominion over the fish of the sea and over the birds of the heavens and over every living thing that moves on the earth."*   —Genesis 1:28

Many would say today that the issues of the world have much more to do with overpopulation than "filling the earth." What we do know is that God has put a high value on providing for our families:

> *But if anyone does not provide for his relatives, and especially for members of his household, he has denied the faith and is worse than an unbeliever.*   —1 Timothy 5:8

Scripture also is clear that it is the parents' role to instruct children in the Lord's ways:

> "You shall love the Lord your God with all your heart and with all your soul and with all your might. And these words that I command you today shall be on your heart. You shall teach them diligently to your children, and shall talk of them when you sit in your house, and when you walk by the way, and when you lie down, and when you rise. You shall bind them as a sign on your hand, and they shall be as frontlets between your eyes. You shall write them on the doorposts of your house and on your gates."
> —Deuteronomy 6:5-9

Two of the qualifications given for prospective leaders in the church—and thus expectations for everyone—are that their children would be obedient to their parents and be following the Lord:

> ... if anyone is above reproach, the husband of one wife, and his children are believers and not open to the charge of debauchery or insubordination.
> —Titus 1:6

One person once said that he believed God was more interested in straight arrows than how many arrows one had. I believe each couple must seek God for how many children they feel they are able to provide for, care for, teach, and raise to be obedient to their parents and to the Lord.

With that said, let's return to the original question. Is it right for married couples to practice family planning? First, let me make the observation that those who do what is called "natural family planning," using the woman's cycle as an indicator of when to be sexually intimate, are using family planning. It is interesting to me that God created women's bodies in such a way that they are not always fertile. If God did not believe it good to have family planning, then why didn't he simply make women fertile all the time? Then women would have children each year from the time of their marriage until they die or are not able to conceive any longer.

I personally do not see anywhere in scripture that it says we are not allowed to make an effort to plan the size of our families. We do know that God is able to overrule any form of family planning we use if He chooses.

Again, to be very clear: family planning is *only* for those who are married. If you are not married, you should not need family planning because you are not to be sexually involved with each other.

Practical Questions: Family Planning

Regarding what form of family planning to use (if you believe it is fine to do this), the only clear direction from scripture we have is in the Psalms, where we read:

> *For you formed my inward parts;*
> *you knitted me together in my mother's womb.* —Psalm 139:13

Therefore, I do not believe we are to use any form of family planning that takes effect after conception, such as a morning-after pill or intrauterine device.

This is a sensitive area, and each couple must seek God's leading for them and be at peace with their decision.

Marriage and Dowries

▨ **Our culture has many traditions surrounding introductions, marriages, church weddings, and dowry. What does scripture teach?**

I am aware this is a very sensitive area and as a non-Ugandan I offer my answer based solely on the principles from God's word. I ask you to seek God, being true to His word first and then sensitive to cultural traditions second.

First, there are a few cases in scripture where bride price or dowry are mentioned, such as Exodus 22:16-17 and Deuteronomy 22:28-29. But we need to make a distinction between what is *described* in scripture, that is, historical accounts, and what is *prescribed*, that is, commandments. For instance, Genesis 29 tells the story of Laban tricking Jacob and substituting Leah for Rachel as his new bride. The account describes what happened, but it is not prescribing what should happen. So it is with many areas recorded in scripture that are not specifically taught in scripture.

Now, here is what we know from scripture. There is a process that is recognized when the husband and wife are "united," literally meaning glued together:

> *Therefore a man shall leave his father and his mother and hold fast to his wife, and they shall become one flesh.* —Genesis 2:24

There is a public and legal recognition that marks when a man and woman are husband and wife. Jesus' first miracle was turning water into wine at a wedding.

In the case of Joseph, the earthly father of Jesus, he was engaged to Mary and yet not married to her, so he was not sexually one with her.

Celebrations were part of Biblical culture, but such celebrations took into account the financial situation of the families. Even with respect to sacrifices at the temple, allowances were made for the financial state of the family so as to not create a hardship on them (see for example, Leviticus 5:7, 5:11, 12:8, and 14:21).

Specifically in Uganda, these would be a few of my observations.

1. Marriage between a man and a woman should be entered into carefully and with good counsel.
2. A couple should be deemed married when they are legally registered as married in the courts.
3. No matter what tradition is celebrated, such as introductions, etc., the couple is not married and therefore are not to be sexually intimate until they are legally married.
4. Those who are Christians should seek to be married in the church and with the blessings of their families and the church body. Where at all possible they should be married by a minister of the gospel.
5. The church should do all it is able to do to help the couple celebrate their wedding in a manner that does not add hardship on the couple or their families.
6. Parents should be encouraged to make sure the man wishing to marry their daughter is a man who is following God, and who is able to support and care for their daughter.
7. I would urge parents and the church to do all it can do to cease the practice of the dowry for the following reasons:
   - The length of time it takes and the pressures on the couple in regards to their sexual purity.
   - The financial pressure it puts on the couple as they start their life together.
   - The implication that the daughter was an object sold and bought. Dowry tends to make the husband feel he "owns" his wife, since he "bought" her. This is contrary to God's word, which clearly states that all persons have equal worth.
   - The resentment towards the parents of the bride, who have made it so difficult for the young couple and have taken the money for their own pleasure rather than supporting the young couple.
   - Children are told by scripture to support their parents, but this is when there is need, which is a very different situation from "paying up front," and thus not having means to help later or refusing to help parents in need due to resentment.

About the Authors

Drs. Paul and Virginia Friesen were married in 1976 and are the parents of three young women, two of whom are now married to wonderful, Godly men. They have been involved in Family Ministries for over 35 years through family camps, church staff positions, speaking, consulting, and writing. In 2003, they founded Home Improvement Ministries (www.HIMweb.org), a non-profit organization dedicated to equipping individuals and churches to better encourage marriages and families in living out God's design for healthy relationships.

As the lead resource couple at Home Improvement Ministries, the Friesens regularly speak at marriage, men's, and women's conferences in the US and internationally, as well as local family and parenting seminars, and have an ongoing ministry with several professional athletic teams. Paul and Virginia both have Doctorates in Marriage and Family Therapy from Gordon-Conwell Theological Seminary.

The Friesens are (with four others) co-authors of the book *Restoring the Fallen* published by InterVarsity Press. Home Improvement Ministries published Paul's book *Letters to My Daughters* in 2006, his book *So You Want to Marry My Daughter?* in 2007, Virginia's book, *Raising a Trailblazer: Rite-of-Passage Trail Markers for Set-Apart Kids* in 2008, and Paul's book *Before You Save the Date* in 2010. They have also co-written two couple-and-small-group marriage guides, *In Our Image: Marriage as a Reflection of the Godhead* (2008) and *Jesus on Marriage* (2012).

Paul and Virginia's greatest joy in life is knowing that their children are walking in the Truth.

Acknowledgments

Special thanks to Derek and Julie Johnson, Miriam Ongom, and Pastors Simon Peter Alelu, Nelson Wacha, and Wilberforce Okumu for your input on this manuscript.

Thank you to the staff from Jenga and CURE Children's Hospital of Uganda for your questions and your desire to seek God's design for relationships.

Thank you to Guy and Barbara Steele for their editing and layout abilities and contributions to this project.

Thank you to the Home Improvement Ministries Board and supporters, who have made it possible for us to minister in Uganda.

Thank you to those who have contributed financially to allow this booklet to be distributed to those who have a deep desire to learn, but have limited finances to purchase such resources.

Finally, and most importantly, a heart full of gratefulness to our Heavenly Father, who designed marriage to reflect His glory—the glory that He experiences in the Trinity.

Resources available from Home Improvement Ministries:

Parenting
Raising a Trailblazer, Virginia Friesen. (book)
Parenting by Design, Paul and Virginia Friesen. (DVD series, with study guide)
The Father's Heart, Paul and Virginia Friesen. (DVD series, with study guide)

Dating, Engagement
Letters to My Daughters, Paul Friesen. (book)
Before You Save the Date, Paul Friesen. (book)
So You Want to Marry My Daughter?, Paul Friesen. (book)
Engagement Matters, Paul and Virginia Friesen. (study guide)

Marriage
Restoring the Fallen, Earl and Sandy Wilson, Paul and Virginia Friesen, Larry and Nancy Paulson. (book)
In Our Image, Paul and Virginia Friesen. (study guide)
Jesus on Marriage, Paul and Virginia Friesen. (study guide)
Recapturing Eden, Paul and Virginia Friesen. (DVD series, with study guide)
Created in God's Image, Paul and Virginia Friesen. (DVD series, with study guide)

Discipleship
Gospel Revolution, Gabriel Garcia. (book)

For more information about Home Improvement Ministries or to order any of our products, please contact us:

Call:	+1 781 275 6473
Email:	info@himweb.org
Write:	Home Improvement Ministries 213 Burlington Road, Suite 101-B Bedford, MA 01730 USA
Online:	www.HIMweb.org/books (for the online bookstore) www.HIMweb.org/speak (to book speakers) www.HIMweb.org/fb (to reach us on Facebook)